Seasons

Winter

Patricia Whitehouse

Heinemann Library
Chicago, Illinois

Customer Service 888-454-2279
Visit our website at www.heinemannlibrary.com

Designed by Sue Emerson, Heinemann Library
Printed and bound in the U.S.A. by Lake Book

07 06 05 04 03
10 9 8 7 6 5 4 3 2 1

Library of Congress Cataloging-in-Publication Data
Whitehouse, Patricia, 1958–
    Winter / Patricia Whitehouse.
       v. cm. — (Seasons)
Includes index.
Contents: What are seasons?—What is the weather like in winter?—What do you wear in winter?—What can you see in winter?—What can you smell in winter?—What can you hear in winter?—What can you taste in winter?—What special things do you do in winter?—Winter quiz.
    ISBN: 1-58810-893-7 (HC), 1-40340-544-1 (Pbk.)
    1. Winter—Juvenile literature. [1. Winter.] I. Title.
(Heinemann Library)
QB637.8 .W48 2003
508.2—dc21

                        2002001166

Acknowledgments
The author and publishers are grateful to the following for permission to reproduce copyright material:
pp. 4. 5 J. A. Kraulis/Masterfile; p. 6 Spencer Grant/PhotoEdit; p. 7 Richard T. Nowitz/Corbis; p. 8 Mary Kate Denny/PhotoEdit; p. 9 Visuals Unlimited; p. 10 Robert A. Flischel/Mira.com; p. 11 Bob Thomas/Stone/Getty Images; p. 12 Warren Stone/Visuals Unlimited; p. 13T William Johnson/Stock Boston; p. 13B Luther C. Goldman/Visuals Unlimited; p. 14 Howard Sokol/Index Stock Imagery, Inc./PictureQuest; p. 15 Gregory A. Williams; p. 16 Robert W. Domm/Visuals Unlimited; p. 17 Dennis McDonald/PhotoEdit; p. 18 Burke/Triolo/Brand X Pictures; p. 19L Laurence Mouton/PhotoAlto; p. 19R Burke/Triolo/Brand X Pictures/PictureQuest; p. 20 Kent Dufault/Index Stock Imagery, Inc./PictureQuest; p. 21L Corbis Stock Market; p. 21R Burke/Triolo/Brand X Pictures/PictureQuest; p. 22 (row 1, L-R) C Squared Studios/PhotoDisc, 22 Ryan McVay/PhotoDisc; p. 22 (row 2, L-R) Siede Preis/PhotoDisc, C Squared Studios/PhotoDisc p. 22 (row 3, L-R) Nancy Sheehan/PhotoEdit, David Toase/PhotoDisc; p. 23 (T-B) C Squared Studios/PhotoDisc, Warren Stone/Visuals Unlimited, Doug Martin/Photo Researchers, Inc., Visuals Unlimited

Cover photograph by Rommel/Materfile
Photo Research by Scott Braut

Special thanks to our advisory panel for their help in the preparation of this book:

Eileen Day, Preschool Teacher
Chicago, IL

Ellen Dolmetsch, MLS
Wilmington, DE

Kathleen Gilbert,
Second Grade Teacher
Austin, TX

Sandra Gilbert,
Library Media Specialist
Houston, TX

Angela Leeper,
Educational Consultant
North Carolina Department
of Public Instruction
Raleigh, NC

Pam McDonald,
Reading Teacher
Winter Springs, FL

Melinda Murphy,
Library Media Specialist
Houston, TX

Some words are shown in bold, **like this.**
You can find them in the picture glossary on page 23.

Contents

What Is Winter?

winter	spring

Winter is a season.

There are four seasons in a year.

In most places, a new season brings new things to see and do.

What Is the Weather Like in Winter?

In most places, it is cold in winter.

There may be icy rain or snow.

In other places, it stays warm in winter.

What Do You Wear in Winter?

In the winter, you wear clothes that keep you warm.

You wear hats and mittens outside.

You may need boots and **snowpants,** too.

What Can You Feel in Winter?

You can feel the cold wind.

You can feel wet snow.

You can feel fuzzy sweaters.

You can feel the heat of a warm fire.

What Can You See in Winter?

You can see smoke coming from chimneys.

You can see your breath when you breathe out.

You may see animals looking
for food.

Sometimes you see birds or squirrels.

What Can You Smell in Winter?

You can smell smoke from the fireplace.

You can smell the wood, too.

You can smell wet mittens drying.

What Can You Hear in Winter?

You can hear snow hitting your window.

You can hear **icicles** falling.

You can hear snow crunch under your boots.

You can hear snow shovels on sidewalks.

What Can You Taste in Winter?

You can taste hot chocolate.

It warms you up after you have been outside.

You can taste warm soup.

You can taste winter treats!

What Special Things Can You Do in Winter?

You can make snow angels.

Flap your arms and move your legs.

You can celebrate special winter holidays.

New Year's Day and Valentine's Day are winter holidays.

Quiz

Which of these clothes do you wear in winter?

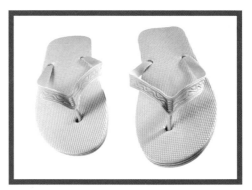

Picture Glossary

boots
pages 9, 17

chimney
page 12

icicle
page 16

snowpants
page 9

Note to Parents and Teachers

Reading for information is an important part of a child's literacy development. Learning begins with a question about something. Help children think of themselves as investigators and researchers by encouraging their questions about the world around them. Each chapter in this book begins with a question. Read the question together. Look at the pictures. Talk about what you think the answer might be. Then read the text to find out if your predictions were correct. Think of other questions you could ask about the topic, and discuss where you might find the answers. Assist children in using the picture glossary and the index to practice new vocabulary and research skills.

Index

24